MONROE TOWNSHIP PUBLIC LIBRARY

D1304064

The Library of the Thirteen Colonies and the Lost Colony[TM]

The Colony of North Carolina

Susan Whitehurst

The Rosen Publishing Group's
PowerKids Press[TM]
New York

For Savannah

Published in 2000 by The Rosen Publishing Group, Inc.
29 East 21st Street, New York, NY 10010

Copyright © 2000 by The Rosen Publishing Group, Inc.

All rights reserved. No part of this book may be reproduced in any form without permission in writing from the publisher, except by a reviewer.

Photo Credits: Cover and title page, pp. 5, 16 © North Wind Pictures, pp. 4, 7, 8, 11, 20 © Granger Collection; p. 12 © Archive & Record Section; p. 19 © Corbis-Bettman.

First Edition

Book Design: Andrea Levy

Whitehurst, Susan.
    The Colony of North Carolina / Susan Whitehurst—1st edition
        p.   cm. — (The library of the thirteen colonies and the Lost Colony)
    Includes index.
    Summary: Traces the history of North Carolina from the arrival of the first European settlers in the mid-seventeenth century through 1789 when it became the twelfth state to join the Union.
    ISBN 0-8239-5485-4
    1. North Carolina—History—Colonial period, ca. 1600-1775 Juvenile literature. 2. North Carolina—History—1775-1865 Juvenile literature.. [1. North Carolina—History—Colonial period, ca. 1600–1775. 2. North Carolina—History— 1775-1865] I. Title. II. Series.
F257.W46 1999
975.6'02—dc21   99-26038
                                                                          CIP
                                                                           AC

J975.602
whi

Manufactured in the United States of America

Contents

Explorers

The story of the colony of North Carolina began in 1584, with an English **explorer** named Sir Walter Raleigh. Raleigh sent ships to Roanoke Island, which is part of North Carolina today. When they arrived, the English asked the Indians who lived there what their country was called. Since the Indians didn't speak English, they didn't understand the question. They said "Wingandacon," which meant "you wear good clothes." The English didn't understand the Indians' language either, so for months they thought the country was called Wingandacon. The English claimed Roanoke and the lands that would later become North Carolina, South Carolina, and Virginia, and said that these lands were now part of England. Queen Elizabeth changed the name of this large area from Wingandacon to Virginia.

◀ *Sir Walter Raleigh first explored the area that would become North Carolina. Later, the city of Raleigh was named after him.*

North Carolina

Roanoke

People in England wanted to know what America was like. Two of Sir Walter Raleigh's sea captains sailed to the part of Virginia called Roanoke Island and brought back animals and plants. Two Native Americans, named Manteo and Wanchese, returned to England with the explorers to help report on what life was like in their land. Since there were no cameras, explorers **hired** artists to draw pictures of the places they visited. Sir Walter Raleigh hired a man named John White to paint pictures of the people and wildlife there. White later became **governor** of the **colony** at Roanoke.

In 1587, White left to get supplies from England. When he returned to the colony, everyone had mysteriously disappeared. Europeans did not return to settle in Roanoke or the rest of the land that is now North Carolina for another 75 years.

To show people back in England what the people of America were like, John White painted this picture of an Indian village. ▶

A Cannow.

The Tuscarora Indians

Before the colonists came, more than 30,000 Indians were already living in the part of Virginia that would later become North Carolina. The Tuscarora were the largest tribe in this area. They lived in longhouses made of wooden poles covered with tree bark. The women farmed corn, beans, and squash. The men hunted and fished. The children gathered berries and nuts and scared birds from the gardens.

The Tuscarora were friendly to the first colonists who came to the land that today is North Carolina. They believed that their god, the Great Spirit, was testing their kindness by sending strangers to their village. When the European settlers started taking over Tuscarora lands, the tribe began to feel differently. After years of being cheated and pushed off their land, the Tuscarora saw the colonists as enemies instead of friends.

The Tuscarora Indians built canoes that they used for fishing and traveling.

Settlers

In 1629, Virginia was divided into two parts, called Virginia and Carolana. Colonists from Virginia came to Carolana looking for good farmland and freedom of religion. In 1663, King Charles's son, King Charles II, gave Carolana to eight family friends. The eight men, called **Lords Proprietors**, divided Carolana into three parts and changed the spelling to Carolina. The northern part was Albemarle County, the beginning of North Carolina.

The name Carolana means "land of Charles" in Latin. King Charles of England named the colony after himself.

Nathaniel Batts built the first house in North Carolina in Albemarle County. Soon, more settlers started coming to Albemarle County. By 1680, over 5,000 people lived there.

King Charles II gave Carolana to eight of his friends. ▷

Lords Proprietors and Culpeper's Rebellion

The Lords Proprietors stayed in England and sent governors to rule Carolina. The Lords Proprietors wanted to make money from the colony. They charged the colonists rent to live in Carolina. The colonists did not like being ruled by lords in England, and they didn't like the governors who cheated them by charging rents that were too high.

In 1677, some farmers in Albemarle County were **smuggling** tobacco to sell in England. When Governor Thomas Miller tried to collect **taxes** for the tobacco, the farmers **rebelled**. Forty colonists, led by John Culpeper, put the governor in jail and ran the colony by themselves for almost two years. It was the first time American colonists had rebelled against England.

◀ *This picture shows Governor Miller in jail. He escaped in 1678 and went back to England.*

Making a Living

By 1690, 8,000 colonists lived in Albemarle County. There were no towns, and almost everyone lived on small farms. Two-thirds of the area that would later become North Carolina was forest. The colonists lived in log cabins and built their furniture out of wood. They grew rice, beans, and potatoes. Their biggest crop was corn. They ate puffed corn, called hominy, for breakfast. They made corn bread, corn cakes, and corn stew. They used corn husks to stuff their mattresses. Corn cobs were fed to the animals. To make money, the settlers grew tobacco to sell to England. They also cut down pine trees to make tar and **turpentine**, which were used in shipbuilding.

North Carolina did not make as much money from tobacco as Virginia did. North Carolina's coast was shallow, so only smaller ships could dock there.

Corn was one of the most important crops in North Carolina. ▶

War and Pirates

In the early 1700s, colonists built two towns in Albemarle County. They built Bath in 1706 and New Bern in 1710. Things seemed to be going well, but a year later, the colony of Carolina almost fell apart.

In 1711, the Tuscarora Indians attacked the colonists. They were angry because the colonists had driven them off their land. The Tuscarora War lasted two years. Thousands of people were killed in the fighting. In the end, the Tuscarora lost the war and their land.

At the same time, Carolina had problems with pirates, who were robbing ships along the coast. The most famous pirate, Blackbeard, lived on Ocracoke Island, near Albemarle.

> Blackbeard sailed up and down the Carolina coast robbing ships. After he was killed in 1718, there were fewer problems with pirates in Carolina.

Blackbeard got his name because he had a black beard that he tied into pigtails. Before a battle, he stuck matches in his hat so that his head would be surrounded by smoke.

Growth and Taxes

In 1712, Carolina was divided into North and South Carolina. In 1729, King George III of England bought North Carolina back from the Lords Proprietors. North Carolina became a royal colony, to be ruled directly by the British government.

The women's rebellion in Edenton, North Carolina was important because it was the first political act by Colonial women against the British government.

Over the next 30 years, North Carolina's population tripled. However, many people who lived there were unhappy. England wanted them to pay more taxes. The colonists did not think it was fair that they had to pay the taxes but did not get to vote in the British government. In the town of Edenton, 50 women gathered and agreed to protest the taxes by refusing to buy English tea and clothes.

The rebellion in Boston, called the Boston Tea Party, encouraged people in other colonies, like North Carolina, to fight against the English taxes. ▶

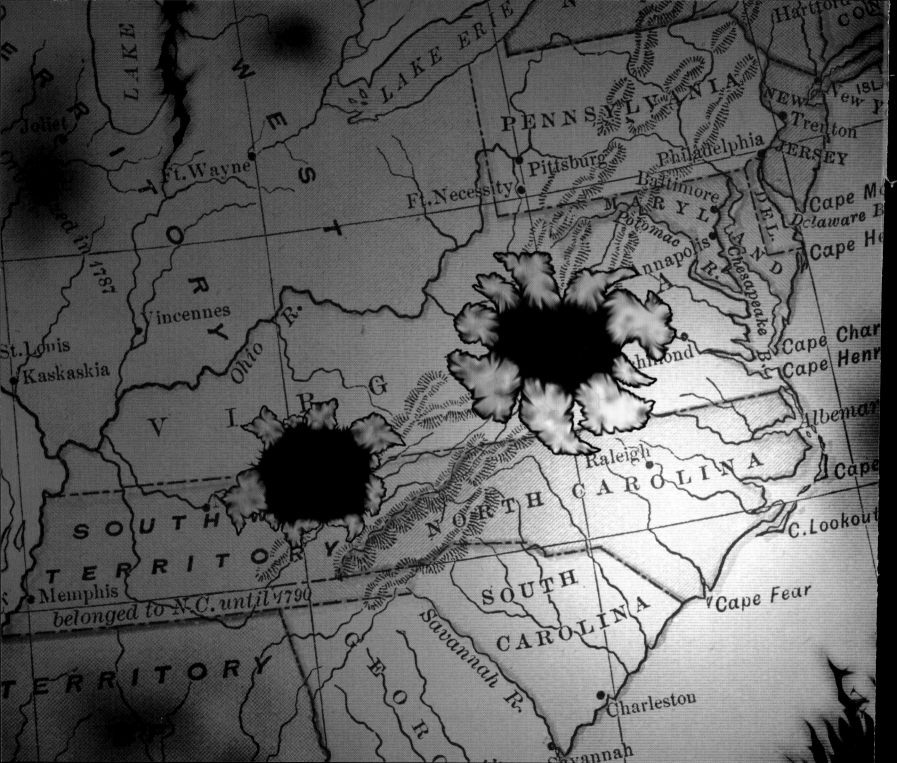

The Revolutionary War

Colonial leaders met in Philadelphia in 1774 to decide what should be done. They asked the king of England to stop taxing the colonies, but he refused. On April 19, 1775, the Revolutionary War began in Massachusetts. About 20,000 men from North Carolina fought in the war. In February 1776, the **Loyalists**, who wanted to remain under English rule, tried to take the town of Wilmington, North Carolina. The **Patriots**, who wanted the colonies to become a new country, soaped and greased the only bridge into town. The Loyalists couldn't get across. The Battle of Moore's Creek Bridge was North Carolina's first Revolutionary War battle.

> In North Carolina's Battle of Moore's Creek Bridge, only one Patriot was killed. Fifty Loyalists were killed, 850 captured, and 2,000 weapons taken.

◀ *A number of Revolutionary War battles were fought in North Carolina.*

Becoming a State

North Carolina was the first colony to vote for **independence** from England, and the twelfth state to join the United States of America. Raleigh, named for Sir Walter Raleigh, became the state's new capital.

After North Carolina approved the Constitution in 1789, they gave a large piece of land to the new government. That land became the state of Tennessee. As a colony, then as a state, North Carolina has always shown its American spirit of both independence and cooperation.

1629		1677		1776	
King Charles I of England divides Carolana from Virginia.	King Charles II gives Carolana to eight Lords Proprietors.	Culpeper's Rebellion.	North Carolina and South Carolina become separate colonies.	Battle of Moore's Creek Bridge.	North Carolina becomes the twelfth state.
	1663		1712		1789

Glossary

colony (KAH-luh-nee) An area in a new country where a large group of people move who are still ruled by the leaders and laws of their old country.

explorer (ik-SPLOR-ur) A person who travels to different places to learn more about them.

governor (GUH-vuh-nur) An official who is put in charge of a colony by a king or queen.

hired (HY-urd) Paid someone to do something.

independence (in-duh-PEN-dints) Making decisions and taking actions without depending on others for direction.

Lords Proprietors (LORDZ pruh-PRY-uh-turz) People who were given a colony for which they made the laws and who could give or sell land to others.

Loyalists (LOY-uh-lists) Colonists who were loyal to their original country and did not want independence from England.

Patriots (PAY-tree-uhtz) Colonists who wanted independence from England.

rebelled (ruh-BELD) Disobeyed the people or country in charge.

smuggling (SMUH-gling) Sneaking something into or out of a country.

taxes (TAK-siz) Money that people give the government to help pay for public services.

turpentine (TUR-pin-tyn) Oil used to thin or dissolve liquids.

Index

Web Sites:

You can learn more about Colonial North Carolina on the Internet. Check out this Web site:

http://www.geocite.com/Athens/Oracle/5650/nc.htm